HAPPY HALLOWEEN!

THINGS TO MAKE AND DO

Written by Robyn Supraner
Illustrated by Renzo Barto

Troll Associates

Library of Congress Cataloging in Publication Data

Supraner, Robyn.
    Happy Halloween.

    SUMMARY: Instructions for making Halloween handi-
crafts for decorations, games, and disguises.
    1. Halloween decorations—Juvenile literature.
2. Handicraft—Juvenile literature. [1. Halloween
decorations. 2. Handicraft. 3. Games] I. Barto,
Renzo. II. Title.
TT900.H32S86   745.594'1   80-23889
ISBN 0-89375-420-X
ISBN 0-89375-421-8 (pbk.)

CONTENTS

GHOSTLY INVITATIONS

Halloween is a time for ghouls and ghosts and witches to gather. Here's an idea for some BOO-tiful invitations for a Halloween party—send them to your favorite goblins!

Here's what you need:

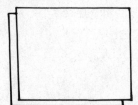
Tracing paper

White drawing paper

Small towel

Push pin

Pencil

Black marker

Tape

Here's what you do:

1 Draw a ghost on a piece of tracing paper. Tape the picture over a sheet of white drawing paper. Put the tracing and the drawing paper on top of a folded towel.

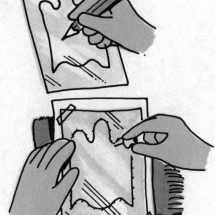

2 Carefully make pinpricks all around the picture. Make them close together. Be sure the pin goes through the drawing paper.

3 Slowly and carefully, tear the ghost shape from the drawing paper.

4 With a black marker, draw a mouth and ghostly eyes.

5 On the front of the invitation write, "WHOOOOOO'S invited to a Halloween party? YOOOOO are!"

6 On the back, write your name, address, and time and date of the party.

PIN THE NOSE ON THE PUMPKIN

Here's an old favorite all dressed up for Halloween.

Here's what you need:

Orange construction paper

White paper

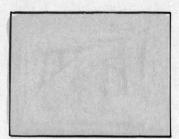
Yellow construction paper

Glue

Cellophane tape

Black marker

Scissors

Here's what you do:

1 Draw a pumpkin on a piece of orange construction paper. *Note:* For a bigger pumpkin, use two pieces of paper taped together.

2 Cut out the pumpkin.

3 From yellow construction paper, cut two eyes and a big, toothy grin for the mouth. Glue these pieces to the pumpkin.

4 Using yellow paper, make a long, triangular nose for each player.

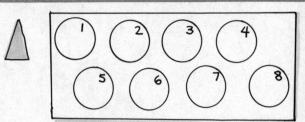

5 On a piece of white paper, draw a circle for each nose. Number the circles. Cut them out. Glue a nose to each circle.

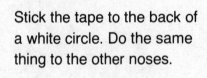

6 Roll a small piece of cellophane tape, sticky side out.

Stick the tape to the back of a white circle. Do the same thing to the other noses.

7 Tape the pumpkin to the wall. Now, you're ready to play. Blindfold each player, and spin him or her around. The player must stick the pumpkin nose to the first place it touches. No matter where! The player who places the nose closest to where it should be is the winner. The one who is farthest away is the booby! Don't forget the prizes!

How does a witch tell time?

She uses a witch watch.

OWL MASK

Here's what you need:

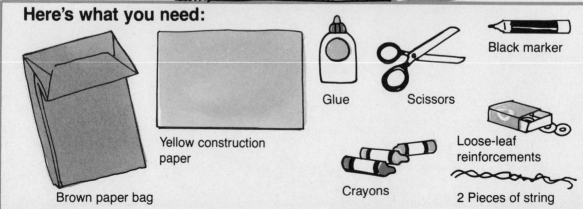

Brown paper bag

Yellow construction paper

Glue

Scissors

Black marker

Crayons

Loose-leaf reinforcements

2 Pieces of string

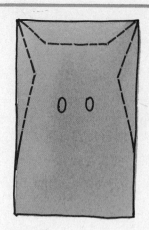

Here's what you do:

1 Cut a large panel from a brown paper bag. Cut around top and side as shown.

2 Hold the mask to your face. With a crayon, mark where to cut holes for the eyes. Gently fold the paper to cut out the eye holes.

3 Draw an oval around each eye hole. Color them orange. Then draw a larger oval around each eye. Color them yellow.

4 Make V-shaped cuts in the mask. Bend them up slightly, so they stick out. These are the owl's feathers.

5 On yellow construction paper, copy this pattern for the owl's beak. Outline it heavily in black. Cut out the beak. Fold it, and glue it in place.

6 Stick a loose-leaf reinforcement to each side of the mask, where it lines up with the top of your eyes. Poke a hole in the brown paper in the middle of each reinforcement. Tie a string to each hole.

What flowers does a goblin grow?

Mari-ghouls and mourning gorys!

11

DANCING SKELETON

Here's what you need:

Large sheet of oak tag or heavy white paper

Scissors

Pencil

String

Black marker

Push pin

14 Paper fasteners

Here's what you do:

1   Use the skeleton shapes on the next two pages. Trace or copy them on a large sheet of oak tag or heavy white paper.

2   With black marker, make a heavy black outline around all the shapes. Then add the eyes, nose, and mouth. If you like, also add lines for the toes, fingers, and ribs.

3   Cut out all the pieces. Join them in the proper order by matching the same color dots together. Use the paper fasteners to join the pieces. Keep them loose, so the pieces can move.

4   Thread a piece of string through the top of the skeleton's head.

5   Jiggle the string up and down and watch the skeleton dance.

6   If you like, take a large cardboard box and cut it as shown. Decorate the sides and use it as a stage.

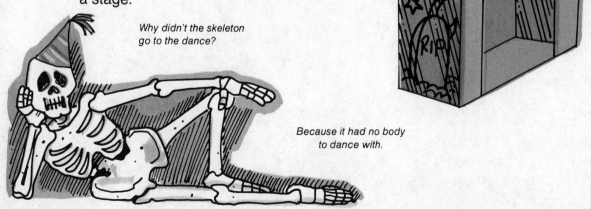

Why didn't the skeleton go to the dance?

Because it had no body to dance with.

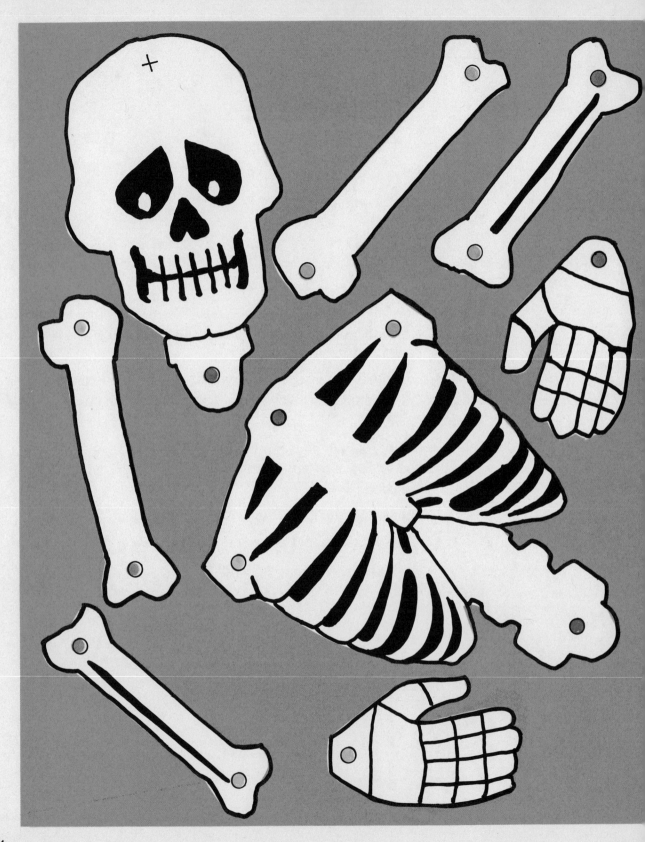

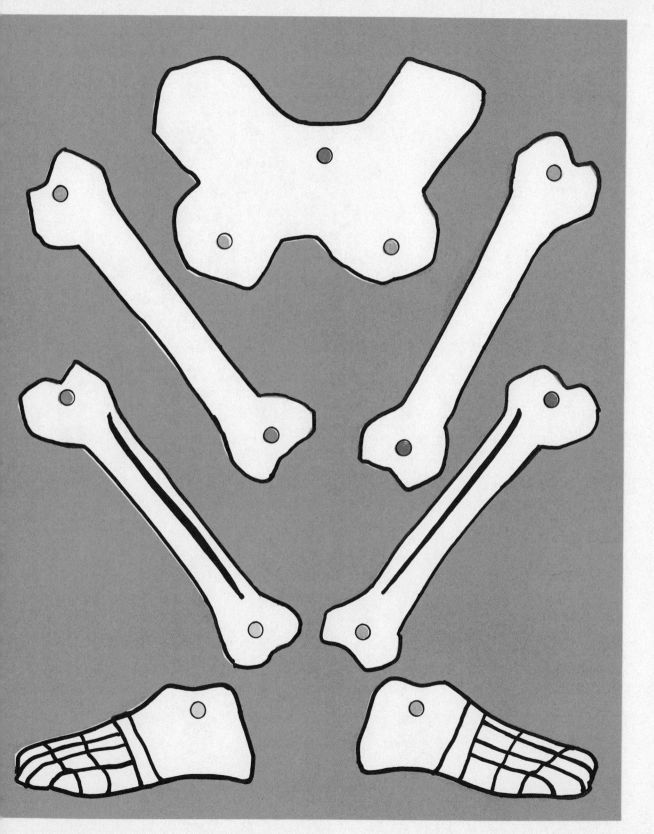

KOOKY CLAY

Here's what you need:

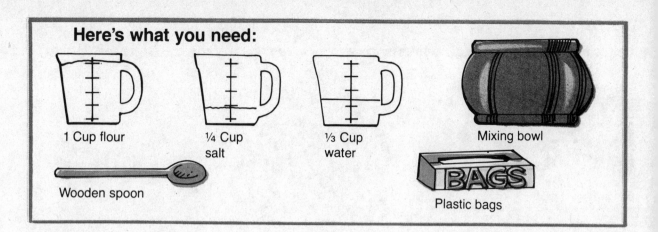

1 Cup flour

¼ Cup salt

⅓ Cup water

Mixing bowl

Wooden spoon

Plastic bags

Here's what you do:

1 Put the flour, salt, and water in a bowl.

2 Mix the ingredients with a wooden spoon. When they are well mixed, press the clay between your fingers to get out any lumps. *Note:* If the clay feels dry and crumbly, add a few drops of water. If it feels too mushy, add a bit of flour.

3 Store the clay in a plastic bag. It will keep for a long time in the refrigerator. Let clay warm to room temperature, before using it.

Kooky Clay is good for making small figures. It can be painted with any water-base paint. You can give the clay a nice shine by brushing a coat of clear nail polish over the paint.

What do witches call little black cats?

Kittens.

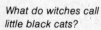

17

HALLOWEEN CHARMS

Here's what you need:

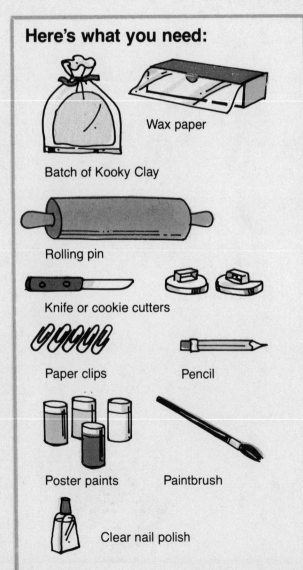

Wax paper

Batch of Kooky Clay

Rolling pin

Knife or cookie cutters

Paper clips

Pencil

Poster paints

Paintbrush

Clear nail polish

Here's what you do:

1   Using a rolling pin, roll out the Kooky Clay on a sheet of wax paper to ¼-inch thick.

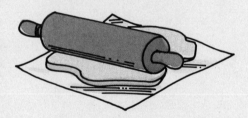

2   With cookie cutters or a knife, cut out a cat, a pumpkin, a ghost, a witch, a vampire, or a bat. Or think of some ideas of your own. These are your Halloween charms.

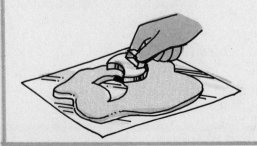

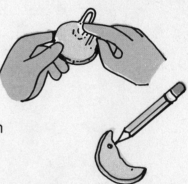

3 Push a paper clip into the back of each charm while clay is still soft. Make sure the top of the clip sticks out above the top of the charm. If the charm is too small for a clip, poke a hole in it with a pencil. Let the charms dry for 2 or 3 days.

4 Decorate each charm with poster paint. Add sequins or beads, too, if you like.

5 Brush on a coat of clear nail polish, after the paint is dry.

6 Tie a charm to a necklace. Dangle one from a bracelet or belt. Attach one to the zipper of your jacket. Hang one from a window shade. Give charms as gifts, or use them for prizes.

Have a CHARMing Halloween!

What happens when a black cat eats a lemon?

It turns into a sour puss.

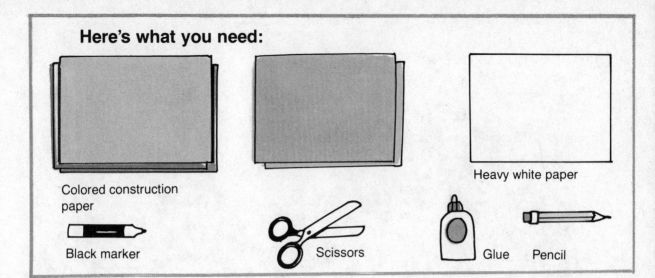

Here's what you need:

Colored construction paper

Heavy white paper

Black marker

Scissors

Glue   Pencil

Here's what you do:

1 Trace the five shapes on the facing page on different colored construction papers. Cut them out.

2 With a black marker, draw eyebrows and mouth on the head.

3 Draw fingernails on the hands. Draw hair and toes on the feet.

4 Glue all the pieces on heavy white paper in the order shown here.

5 When the glue is dry, cut out the bookmark monster.

6 Draw in two eyes. Put the monster in a book with its head and feet sticking out.

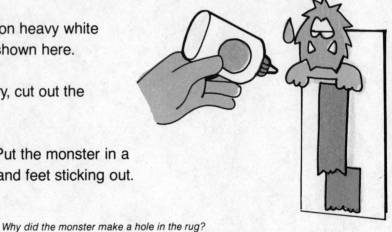

Why did the monster make a hole in the rug?

It wanted to see the floor show.

WANDA WITCH: A PUPPET OR MASK

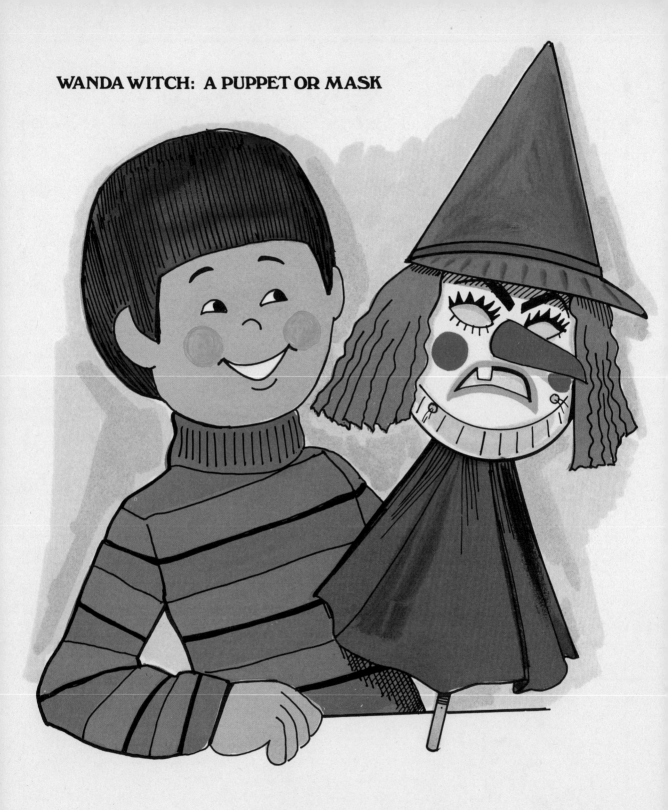

Here's what you need:

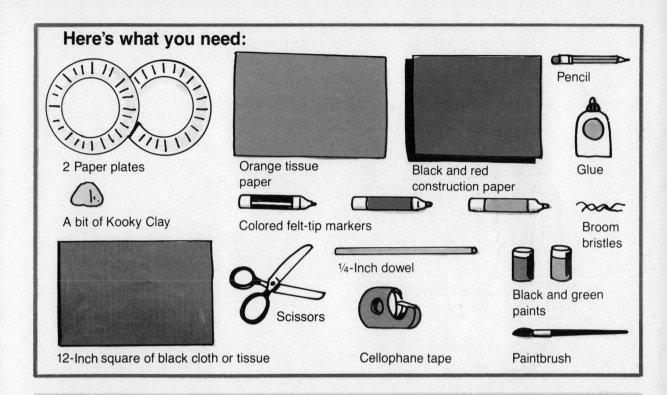

2 Paper plates

A bit of Kooky Clay

Orange tissue paper

Colored felt-tip markers

Black and red construction paper

Pencil

Glue

Broom bristles

12-Inch square of black cloth or tissue

Scissors

¼-Inch dowel

Cellophane tape

Black and green paints

Paintbrush

Here's what you do:

1   Hold a paper plate up to your face and mark where to cut holes for the eyes, nose, and mouth.

2   Cut two holes for eyes. Cut a circle, about the size of a quarter, for the nose. Cut out a mouth with one tooth sticking out.

3   Outline the eyes with a black marker. Draw pointy eyelashes. Draw mean eyebrows.

4   Draw a wicked mouth with green pen.

5   Make red circles for the cheeks with red pen.

6 Cut the other plate in half. Paint one half black. (Save the other half for another project.)

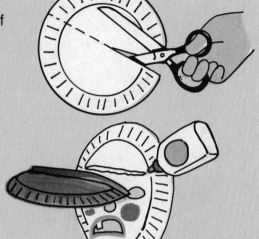

7 When it's dry, fold the cut edge up, and glue it to the mask just above the eyes. This is the brim of the witch's hat.

8 Cut a large triangle from black construction paper. Glue it above the brim. This is the top of the witch's hat.

9 Cut strips of orange tissue paper for hair. Crumple each strip, and glue it to the mask.

10 Divide the Kooky Clay into three small balls. Stick a few broom bristles into each ball. These are the witch's warts! Set them aside to dry. When the warts are dry, paint them black and green, and glue them to the mask.

11 With scissors, snip a tiny hole in the center of the black cloth or tissue paper, just big enough for the dowel to fit through. Tape the dowel and cloth to the back of the plate. The dress will hide your hand as you move the puppet about. For a mask, hold Wanda's face in front of your own.

12 Use this pattern for Wanda's nose. Use red construction paper. Roll it into a cone shape, and glue it. Bend the tabs up. Place it in the nose hole of the mask, and tape the tabs to the inside.

Why was Wanda the best in her class?

Because she was the best speller!

Here's what you need:

Pipe cleaners

Pencil

Glue

Scissors

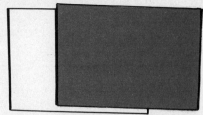

White and red construction paper

Here's what you do:

1 Fold a sheet of white paper in half. Place your wrist on the fold in the paper and trace around your hand. Cut out the hand. Cut through both halves of the paper, but leave the paper attached at the fold.

2 Cut five long fingernails from red paper. Glue them on one of the hands.

3 Place a pipe cleaner through a small hole in the fold line, and glue along the middle finger. Glue lengths of pipe cleaner to each finger.

4 Glue the hands together. Bend the fingers so the hand looks *extra* creepy-crawly. Creepy-crawlies look good crawling out of drawers and closets. They also make good bookmarks. The pipe cleaner will keep your place.

Why do creepers crawl?

Because they never learned to walk.

MUSICAL JELLY BEANS

Here's what you need:

Jelly beans

Record

Record player

Musical Jelly Beans is a good game to play at a Halloween party. It is played like Musical Chairs.

Here's what you do:

1 Line up the players and start the music.

2 While the music is playing, the players must pass the jelly beans from hand to hand.

3 When the music stops, the player holding the jelly beans is out of the game. The music is started and stopped until only one player is left. The winner gets a bag of jelly beans. *Remember:* It is not fair to eat the jelly beans when you are caught holding them!

When is it bad luck to have a black cat cross your path?

When you are a mouse.

29

Here's what you need:

Black paper

White pencil

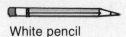
Scissors

Orange
cellophane

Cellophane tape

Hole punch
(optional)

Here's what you do:

1 Draw lots of bats on black paper,
using a white pencil. Make big bats
and small bats. Cut out the bats.

2 Cut round holes for their
eyes, or use a hole punch.

3 Tape a bit of orange
cellophane behind the eyes.

4 If you do not have a belfry, hang your bats in a window. When the sun
shines in, their eyes will light up! *Note:* A belfry is a bell tower. Some bats
make their homes in belfries.

If you threw a black bat into the Red Sea, what would it become?   Wet!

31

WHOOOOO AM I?

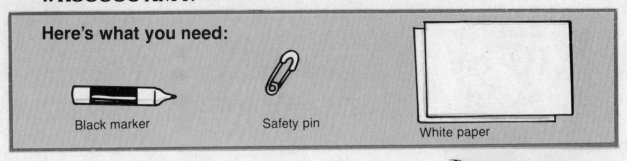

Here's what you need:

Black marker

Safety pin

White paper

Here is another game to play on Halloween.

Here's what you do:

1 Write a word that has something to do with Halloween on a piece of paper. Make up as many sheets of paper, each with a different word, as there are players. Some good words are BAT, GHOST, WITCH, BROOM, JACK-O-LANTERN, BLACK CAT, VAMPIRE, PUMPKIN, GHOUL, GOBLIN, and SKELETON.

2 To start the game, the players sit in a circle. Choose someone to be "it." The player who is "it" stands in the middle of the circle with one of the words pinned to her or his back.

3 Everyone knows the word except the player who is standing in the circle. The player tries to find out "WHOOOOO AM I?" by asking twelve questions. The questions must be answered "yes" or "no." After twelve questions, it is someone else's turn. This game has no winner. It's just fun to play!

What would you get if you crossed a laughing hyena with a black cat?

A giggle puss!

COUNT DRACULA PUPPET

Here's what you need:

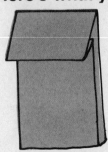

Small bag

Black marker

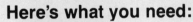

Scissors

Glue

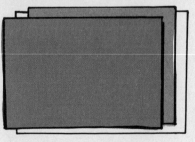

White and colored papers

Here's what you do:

1 Cut out two teeth and shirt front from white paper. Cut out mouth and shirt sash from red paper. Glue to bag as shown.

2 Cut out two dark-blue pieces for cape and jacket. Fold as shown and glue in position.

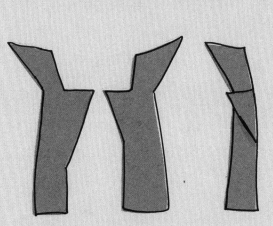

3 Cut out a circle for a monocle, and glue it on face. With black marker, draw an eye on the circle. Draw the other eye on the bag. Add two dots for nose, black hair, eyebrows, and tie.

4 Put your hand inside the bag. Open and close your hand to open and close Count Dracula's mouth.

COOKIE MONSTERS

Here's what you need:

Marshmallows

Chocolate bits

Candy corn

Cookie sheet

Cookies

2 Pot holders

Here's what you do:

1 Preheat oven to 350°.

2 Place the cookies on a cookie sheet.

3 Decorate the cookies with marshmallows, chocolate bits, and candy corn. Make goblins, ghosts, and ghouls! Make scary faces! Use the faces on the next two pages, or create your own.

4 Put the cookie sheet into the oven for about 5 minutes or until the candy gets soft and starts to melt.

5 Use pot holders to take the cookie sheet out of the oven. Wait until the cookies cool, or eat them while they are warm.

Note: If you are not allowed to use the oven, ask a grownup to help you.

What do you drink with cookie monsters?

Ghoul-Aid.

37

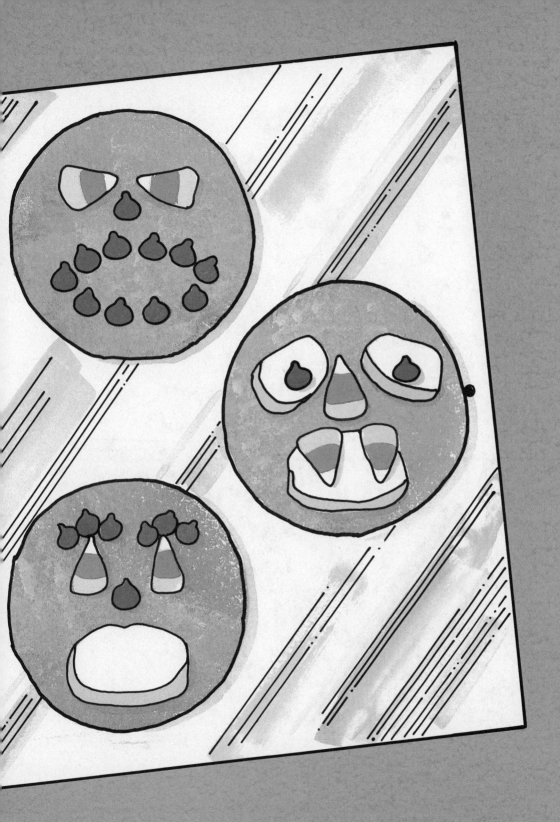

TRICK OR TREAT HALLOWEEN BAG

Here's a bag for "Trick or Treat" with a place for your special treasures.

Here's what you need:

Loose-leaf reinforcements

Large bag

Small bag

Glue

Heavy yarn or string

Crayons

Scissors

Colored paper

Here's what you do:

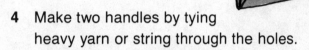

1 Stick two loose-leaf reinforcements on each side of a big bag. Stick them near the top, about 6 inches apart.

2 Punch a hole in the center of each reinforcement.

3 Open the bag, and stick a reinforcement on the other side of each hole.

4 Make two handles by tying heavy yarn or string through the holes.

5 Print the word "Treasure" on a small bag. Glue the small bag to one side of the big bag. Use enough glue to hold it tight.

6 Decorate the bags in any way you like. Cut cats and bats and witch's hats from black paper. Stick on stars and moons. Use crayons and bits of colored paper. Use your imagination!

What is the last thing a witch takes off before she goes to bed?

She takes her feet off the floor.

Front

Back

THE WITCH'S CALDRON

Try this game at your next Halloween party.

Here's what you need:

 A cup and 25 jelly beans

 Iron caldron (if you don't have a caldron, use a big pot)

Here's what you do:

1 Put the caldron on the floor or on a low table.

2 Each player takes a turn trying to throw the jelly beans into the caldron.

3 The player with the most jelly beans is the winner. Remember to stand about 10 feet away from the caldron. Also remember to toss only one jelly bean at a time!

How do you make a witch scratch?

Take away her "W."

MONSTER MOBILE

Here's what you need:

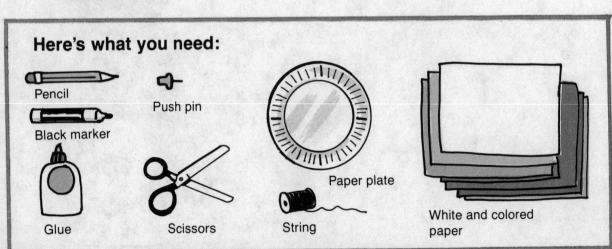

Pencil

Push pin

Black marker

Glue

Scissors

String

Paper plate

White and colored paper

Here's what you do:

1 Cut the string into 6 pieces. Cut 2 pieces, 12 inches long. Cut 2 pieces, 10 inches long. Cut 2 pieces, 8 inches long.

2 Poke 6 holes around the edge of a paper plate. Make the holes about 4½ inches apart.

3 Tie a piece of string through each hole. Let the ends of the strings hang down.

4 Cut 6 monster shapes from colored paper. Decorate both sides of each monster. Decorate them any way you like. *Here are some suggestions:* Make the eyes with white and black paper. Loose-leaf reinforcements make good eyes, too. Make a 3-eyed monster! Make big ears. Make big noses. Make big teeth! Make a BLOB! Make a THING! Make one of these monsters or create some of your own.

5 Poke a hole in the top of each monster, and tie it to a string on the paper plate.

6 Attach the mobile to the top of a doorway with a push pin. The monsters will move when there is a breeze.

What should you say when you meet a two-headed monster?

Hello. Hello.

How do you get rid of a yellow monster?

Scare it away.

What kind of raincoat does a purple monster wear?

A wet one.

How do you catch a blue monster?

With a blue-monster net.

How do you catch a red monster?

Hold its nose until it turns blue, then catch it with a blue-monster net.

47